Maybe: A Collection of Thoughts, Musings, and Nonsense

Melanie Davis

Presentation by *BookLeaf Publishing*

Web: www.bookleafpub.com

E-mail: info@bookleafpub.com

ISBN: 9789358311884

First edition 2023

To my husband, Lee, who has been encouraging my writing for so long and is the best inspiration and support. I love you!

ACKNOWLEDGEMENTS

Thank you to my family, my friends, and all the people in my life who make me laugh. Laughing and discussing and thinking and postulating is my favorite way of learning more about others and myself. Thank you specifically to Lee, Tim, Julie, Mary, Jeremy, Jasmine, Matthew, Bob, Casey, Emma, Millie, Beau, Katherine, Megan, Susie, and Emily, Becca, and Sandy: The Women's Council. I love you all so much. Thank you for encouraging me and loving me so well.

PREFACE

As a High School English Teacher, and later an AP Lit Teacher, I already loved poetry. When I found a chance to write my own book of poetry and publish it, I couldn't say no. Then the question became, what do I write about? This writing challenge happened in July 2023, so would there be a fireworks poem? Something about independence? Starting a new school year? Maybe. Would it be about being halfway through my Master's Degree, back in college for the first time in 20 years? Maybe. Could it be about other things? Books I'm reading? Dates with my husband? Vacation? Existential Dread? Maybe. Now you know how the title came to be. In saying, "Maybe," we say, "There's a chance." Or "I'll think about it." Or "Not 'Yes,' but not 'No.'" As I look at the second half of my Degree, the almost-second-half of my career, and definitely the almost-second half of my life, I am in a state of Maybe. Considering all the angles, all the options, finding options and angles I hadn't even thought existed yet, and pausing. So, that's what I hope for you, dear reader: may you pause, consider, explore, and say, "Maybe," when you haven't made up your mind, and maybe you'll know that's okay.

-M. Davis

How Many Seconds Do You Need?

I live in a 20 second city;
even when the
light is green,
I sit for 20 seconds
because the traffic is
so
bad.
I miss 1 second cities —
Fewer people,
fewer buildings,
fewer stressors.
Or 5 second cities
where you
waited just a couple
to let a dog cross
with its human
or say hello
to a neighbor…
not to stare at skyscrapers
and moan about the heat.
Perhaps I'll find a
3 second city
A happy medium
Giving me a taste of life

But leaving me
to my thoughts
more often
than not.
Good for thinking,
Bad for networking,
Good for thoughts,
Bad for conversation,
When we have
too many seconds
We need thirds
And fourths…
I want to learn
Moderation, but I'm sometimes
Selfish
Oops! Time to go
The light is green.

Untraditional

Instead of a cake,
Pecan pie.
Instead of singing,
Laughter.
(But if we sing,
It's 3 part harmony,
At least.)
Finding something you'd
Love lots
And
Use often.
Whether it's the way
People think it should be
Or not,
The most important tradition
Is to celebrate you.
Happy Birthday, Dad!

Or

Stiffness
Soreness
Heavy breathing
Redness in the face
May be from
A lack
Of movement
Or
An abundance
Of movement
Crying
Laughing
Screaming
Jumping
May be from
A lack of joy
Or
An abundance
Of joy
Staring
Steady breathing
Head cocked
Hand out
May be from
A lack

Of concentration
Or
An abundance
Of Concentration
Perspective informs us
Gives us tools to assess our surroundings
Did you blink?
Or flinch?
Did you smile?
Or grimace?
Should I say, "Congratulations!"
Or
"I'm so so sorry!"
Possibly, "Look out!"
Or
"Quick! This way!"
Be sure to look
Before you jump
And if you don't,
Plan the landing accordingly

Cotton Candy Angel Hair

Not many people
have a favorite
type of firework.
I do!
I don't even know what the
official
name is for it,
but I call it "angle hair,"
like the pasta.
This firework has a huge diameter
and spokes of varying lengths,
all super thin
streaks of light.
And when all the streaks
have reached
the end
of their journey,
each
tiny
spark
just
hovers.
Then they sparkle.
They twinkle.
They do not fall.

They just twinkle away
and disappear,
like those dandelion puffs,
like wisps of cotton candy.
That's another good name:
Cotton Candy Angel Hair.
Sweet.
Simple.
Here for a good time,
not for a long time,
but lasts in my memory.
Just twinkle,
twinkle,
twinkle,
fade.
And then light it up again!

Prompts

Writing prompts can help you
Get out of a funk.
Sometimes they give you gems,
Sometimes they give you junk.

But even if your writing
Makes you say oof, ack, and ouch,
You're proverbially lapping
Everyone on the proverbial
Writing couch.

Full Circle

When I was younger,
and my family visited
my grandma's,
(We called her Mama Lu
-she said she was
too young looking
to be called
grandma)
It was not too long
before we started asking
when our favorite cousins
could come over,
Or when we could
go over there,
Or when our "cool" aunts and uncles
were coming over,
(we had so many
cool aunts and uncles!)
Or when we could
go over there.
Dad was in the Air Force,
So we moved a lot,
But going to Florida was "Going Home."
We loved visiting family!
Having sleepovers

Going to the store to buy snacks
Getting milkshakes
Putting on shows on
Mama Lu's back porch
Laughing and eating ice cream
'till our stomachs hurt
(we weren't sure if it was
the jokes
or
the ice cream!)
Magic tricks from Uncle Ron before bed
It was a time of making
many core memories!
Now, when my brother's kids
come to visit my mom,
(They call her Mama Lu;
she says she looks
too young
to be called grandma.
My Mama Lu
is now
"Mama Lu 2" or
"Great Mama Lu" or
even "GiGi" to her
great grands!)
They ask, "When are Aunt Mel and Uncle Lee
coming over?"
"Can Jasmine and Matthew
come swim with us?"

"Can we go over to Aunt Mary and Uncle Jer's?"
We were once
the cousins who visit.
Now we are
the cool Aunts and Uncles
who are excited
for the cousins
to visit.
We are still making core memories:
Swimming in Mama Lu and Papa Lu's pool
Playing cards for packets of Stevia
Weaving baskets
Arts and Crafts with Aunt Mel
Still laughing till our stomachs hurt
It is so special to be in a
Full
Circle
Moment

And appreciate
the many roles
family can fill
Someday maybe Jasmine, Emma, and Millie
will be the cool Aunts
Beau and Matthew, cool uncles
Maybe Casey
will be a Mama Lu,
Or Bob
could be a Papa Lu.
What will they call Mar and Jer?

There may be
cousins to visit
Or cousins who visit
And we will
Come full circle
Again

A Trip to the Bookstore

It seems like a simple pleasure
The bookstore
But inside are
countless adventures
Journeys
into the sea or space
Conundrums
taking years to solve
Protagonists
finding euphoria and despair
Antagonists
planning downfalls and traps
And we enter
unaware of our possibilities
Looking for a specific book
Looking for a specific genre
Looking for a general how-to
Looking
In seeking we shall find
More than we ever thought possible
We may enter
and find one immediately
Looking at other options
But sticking with
our first gut instinct

We may enter with
no particular choice in mind
Browsing
Taking pictures of covers
Weighing our options
and budget
And choose a new adventure
Eventually
We may read our book in the space of
an hour
Or an afternoon
Or a day
Or a week
And when we are finished
We go back to the bookstore
For more journeys
For more problems to be solved
For more protagonists for whom we cheer
For more villains we love to hate
For more
And find worlds we never would have found
Without
A trip to the bookstore

Balance

I have so many
Chores
Responsibilities
Obligations
"Should"s
But I have no
Motivation
Get-up-and-go
Oomph
Vim, vigor, and vitality
"Would"s
I feel
Bored
Overwhelmed
Tired
Meh
And that's okay
If we had all the motivation
in every day,
would we be motivated to rest?
Is motivation only for activity?
Can I be vigorously
staring into space?
Is a brain break full
of vitality?

I propose a merger.
A partnership, if you will
The need for both
Motivation
And
"Meh"-tivation
The ability to truly check out
Zone out
Space out
Even freak out!
All of these phrases include "out"
We take a step
Outside our responsibilities
Outside our comfort zone
Outside our rat race mentality
So we can
Tune in
Into what we really need
Into how we really feel
Into what we know for sure
Sometimes we have to zone out
to focus in
Rest is not earned
But it is necessary
Tasks are not required
Until they are
Balance is key,
both in work and
In leisure

So that we can appreciate our efforts in both
I am proud of my rest
I am proud of my work
Both are important
Both are necessary
One does not
earn the other
Lazy does not exist
Choices are
the only currency
Choosing one
neglects the other
Consequences
result naturally
Accepting them
(and adjusting accordingly)
Produces balance
That is the true goal: balance
So I will nurture my Mehtivation
Until I reach a place
to engage my
Motivation
And balance my ability
to succeed
in both

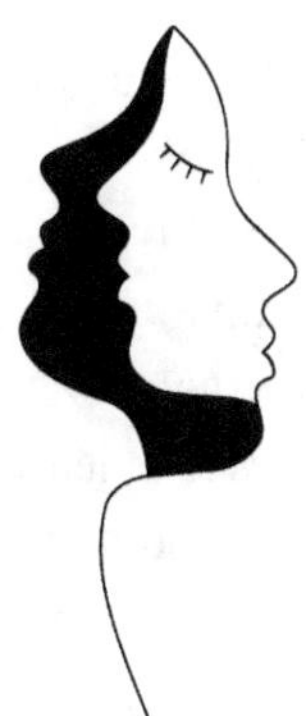

Books

They are gateways
Mirrors
Windows
Paths
Miracles
Lessons learned in ways
We couldn't learn at home
Journeys to places
We could not experience
any other way
This may be just the
English Teacher Talking
But my life would be
Incomplete
Boring
Muted
Lackluster
Dreadful
Dragging
And just plain sad
Without Books

Swords or Pens

William Shakespeare once wrote,
"The pen is mightier than the sword"
But is it?
Truly there are feats
a pen can accomplish
that a sword
cannot,
but the opposite is also true.
Pens craft treaties,
constitutions,
love letters and resignations.
However, swords fight wars,
defeat enemies,
defend lovers, and resign lives.
I guess they're on equal footing,
but that's
not as eloquent,
is it?

Like a Girl

When did "like a girl"
become an insult?
Especially in the
subtext of a tampon commercial?!
When did "like a man"
become a challenge?
Why do we
prove men's
strength
with fists
and women's
with fragility?

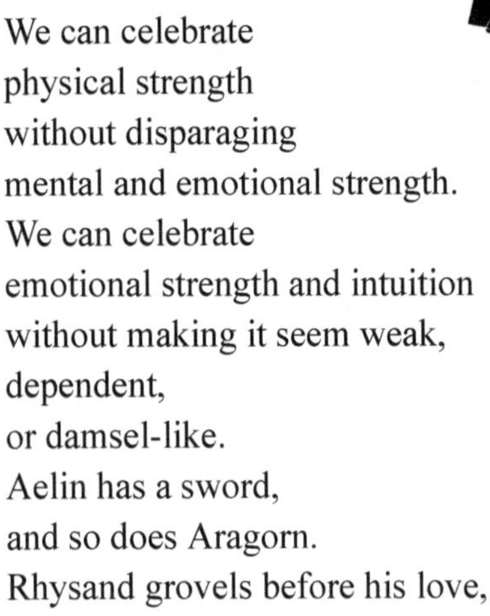

We can celebrate
physical strength
without disparaging
mental and emotional strength.
We can celebrate
emotional strength and intuition
without making it seem weak,
dependent,
or damsel-like.
Aelin has a sword,
and so does Aragorn.
Rhysand grovels before his love,

as does Ophelia.
Maybe it doesn't have
to be done "like a man"
to be seen as strong.
Maybe it can be
accomplished "like a girl"
with grace and tenderness.
And
vice
versa.

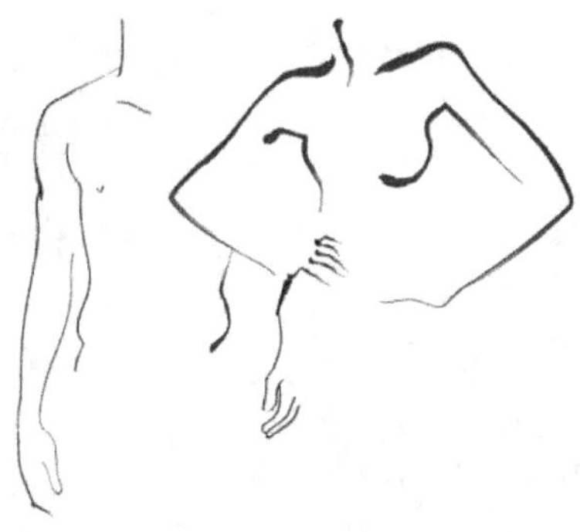

Carrying On

Sometimes
when we see something
huge,
sky-encompassing,
it's so broad and bright
we cannot help but
gaze at it.
Sometimes
that's not the whole story.
We may think
we know
everything
about a situation
but actually know
almost nothing.
Perspective is so key
to learning and growing and changing.
Without it we
stagnate and perish,
never knowing
what else was
out there to learn.

Brainstorming

Getting together.
A meeting of minds.
A heart-to-heart.
Fizzy drinks and pastries
as we solve
all the world's problems.
Well, maybe not all of them.
Someone has
an amazing idea,
that leads to
someone else's additionally
amazing idea.
And another.
And another.
Like dominoes,
but with purpose
and growth!
We notice the rain
outside the cafe.
Torrential,
sheets running down windowed doors,
loud thunder and bright lightening
even though the sun has not set.
I guess we really did
have a brainstorming session!

Haiku Collection

There are times that I
Wish that I could stop time, but
I would miss the rush.

Procrastination
Always gets me into jams.
Peanut butter! Yum!

Reading and writing
Have always been my escape
Flying in my mind.

Sleep

We need it every night.
Without it we struggle.
Thoughts fuzzy,
Feet sluggish,
Face scrunched,
Eyes slitted,
Too much sometimes also sucks.
Throwing off schedules,
Trashing plans,
Wasting daylight.
Happy mediums do exist,
They're just hard to find
When
      You're
            Drifting
                 Off.

Venus de Milo

There are times when
I am struggling.
People pleasing is a
vacuum with no capacity.
One never has to change the bag
on perfectionism.
It just keeps sucking energy,
making us second-guess
our choices,
comments,
facial expressions,
even texts!
"Did I say that too sarcastically?"
"Oh no, did that sound like I was bad mouthing
her?"
"Was I bad mouthing her??"
Candid photos reveal
a resting bored face,
not engaged,
even though I know I was paying attention.
These are the thoughts that
haunt my brain:
    A. when I'm trying to be useful
    B. When I'm trying to focus on my family
    C. When I'm trying to sleep

D.   Trying to contribute.
E.   Trying.
(Usually E. All of the Above)
Then
there are times I feel competent,
useful, and needed.
Essential, even!
I have helpful ideas!
People laugh at my jokes!
I'm their favorite.
But then there's
a "different vibe."
Seemingly without reason,
their faces change.
and I don't have anything to say.
and I say the wrong thing.
and the trying doesn't change,
and it's not my fault,
but it feels like it is.
It's like all of a sudden
my arms have been cut off
as I turn to stone.
Frozen in anxiety and indecision.
So I wait.
To see how it's going to go.
To reach for that happy medium
between perfectionism and success.
To aim for the best,
but have a plan B,

and C,
and D,
and E None of the above.
and I plan,
and revise,
and edit,
and circle back,
and rethink.
Sometimes it's enough,
Sometimes it works,
Sometimes it doesn't.

It's hard to know what to do with no arms.

But even statuesque
With missing limbs
I remember:
I am enough.
So I break out of the freeze,
Gather up my limbs,
And try again tomorrow.

Adulthood

Vacuuming
Washing dishes immediately
Appreciating a clean sink
Counter space
Being excited
to buy new appliances
This is my life now.
I once went out dancing
till 4 am
Then ate at an All Star
before sleeping 4 hours,
Getting up in time
for my 11 am Bio class,
(Which I got a D+ in, by the way…
Do with that information what you will…)
Now that same All Star is too much
Too greasy
Too many carbs
Too many calories
They don't tell you that
as you get too old for some things,
some things become too much
As we get older,
we think we will know more,
do more,

understand more,
But maybe we just understand
what we don't know
even more…
Knowing that we still have
room to grow
To learn
To change
Even in Adulthood
That's the real wisdom that comes.
Someone once said, "We are not cakes;
We are not fully baked."
Shhhh don't tell the youths!
It's a secret.

Encouragement

"It falls out of you like gravity...,"
my husband says,
as he gapes at my writing, my poetry.
I smile
and say, "Thank you!"
Beaming with pride and excitement.
I have not always
accepted encouragement so easily.
I sometimes surprise myself
when I reread
what I've written,
as if I embody
someone else entirely
during the writing process
and surface into the first persona,
to be wowed and impressed by...
myself,
just a different version of myself.
Ernest Hemingway supposedly once said, "Write
drunk; edit sober."
While I don't follow that advice
to the letter,
I think I understand it in spirit:
writing is a totally different animal
than any refinement that comes afterward.

The writer and editor may
have the same body,
but they are not the same
mind, heart, or spirit.
And we need both!
The writers: wild and passionate idea makers,
writing down the beautiful, detailed,
complicated, world-changing information.
The editors:
organizing, categorizing, revising,
grammar correcting, punctuating,
communicating the writer's ideas
well and fully.
And both need encouragement.
Which is easy for people to give
the wild idea maker,
But it's not as easy to see the need in the editor,
but both are part of our writing process.
Both are needed.
Both matter.
I am both.

So Many

There are so many options
we have in life,
but only so many opportunities
to choose.
As we travel our
different paths in life,
some will choose avenues
we may not have.
Choose journeys we wish
would have been available to us
and are not.
Choose roads that
we never even considered.
But we must remember that
our choices are often
exponential.
So are our non-choices.
Choose carefully;
choose wisely,
and plan your next choice with thought.
We only have
so many.

School Year Prep

I need to arrange desks
in my classroom;
My students will be here
before I know it!
Make last minute school supply lists,
Start meeting with teams
about this year's lessons,
(Some of those teams
Are just me…)

I have so many
posters to hang
Chairs to move
Boxes to unpack…
Moving is rough!
Closet to closet,
Wall to wall,
Drawer to drawer.

As I look towards
how this year will go,
I'm so excited
to meet new people
to try new things
to do my best

to ensure
These students
walk away with a positive experience
in my classroom.

No matter what number
is on the door
The people inside
matter more.

Word Associations

The first time you were able,
and I didn't have a chance,
you said that I would have
a good day.

The weather wasn't good today,
but the sun is still shining
on my house,
so I'm going for the night,
to see how the sun works.

This is the only way I know,
(if it has to do something with it,
and it doesn't have a chance
of being a good thing),
but it's a great way
of getting people out there.

I think they need
a little more help
from you guys
than they do.
The rest is the same thing
that they need from the community:
to help out

and know
they are very good people.

The only problem
with the game
was the fact the player
had a bad reputation
and the player
had no choice and
he had no right of doing that
and the player didn't want him
in his place
so they had a choice.

Word association
is a revealing look
at thoughts inside your phone.
Hit the middle button again and again.
What do you learn about your own?

www.ingramcontent.com/pod-product-compliance
Lightning Source LLC
La Vergne TN
LVHW010827200726
843508LV00012B/2524